MW01687884

THE GREAT AUSTRALIAN HOME BREW BOOK

Making great beer at home can be as enjoyable as drinking it. This book tells you how. Specially written for Australians, and using locally available equipment and ingredients, it tells everything, from how to make better beer from Brew Kit Cans, to how to make your own beers to suit your own taste.

XXX

THE GREAT AUSTRALIAN HOME BREW BOOK

Douglas Stewart & Russell McKenzie

Angus&Robertson
An imprint of HarperCollins*Publishers*

This book is dedicated to all our friends and acquaintances, who unstintingly gave much of their time sampling our beers, and to our wives who put up with it all, and cleaned up afterwards.

AN ANGUS & ROBERTSON BOOK
An imprint of HarperCollinsPublishers

First published in New Zealand in 1991
First published in Australia in 1992 by
CollinsAngus&Robertson Publishers Pty Limited (ACN 009 913 517)
A division of HarperCollinsPublishers (Australia) Pty Limited
25–31 Ryde Road, Pymble NSW 2073, Australia

HarperCollinsPublishers (New Zealand) Limited
31 View Road, Glenfield, Auckland 10, New Zealand

HarperCollinsPublishers Limited
77–85 Fulham Palace Road, London W6 8JB, United Kingdom

Text copyright © Douglas Stewart 1991
Drawings copyright © Russell McKenzie

This book is copyright.
Apart from any fair dealing for the purposes of private study, research, criticism or review, as permitted under the Copyright Act, no part may be reproduced by any process without written permission. Inquiries should be addressed to the publishers.

ISBN 0 207 17573 X

Designed by Russell McKenzie, Avenue Graphics
Typeset by Jacobsons Graphic Communications
Printed in Hong Kong

5 4 3 2 1
95 94 93 92

Contents

About this book...

Welcome. You are about to join one of the world's fastest growing clubs, Home-brewers International. All you need is a glass of your favourite in your hand and you are a member.

Home-brewing's growing popularity can be explained by three important things you'll soon discover. One, it is easy. Two, it is cheap. Three, the beer is great. That is why over 30% of all the beer enjoyed in the UK and about 8% in Australia is being brewed at home by people like yourself.

As a brewer you follow in the footsteps of the ancient Egyptians who made one of mankind's great discoveries, how to make beer, before the pyramids were built. Indeed, beer may have played a vital role in sustaining morale during construction. Many claim this same theory applies to lawnmowing in our own time!

Undoubtedly your friends have told you horror stories about dreadful brews of yesteryear, three-year hangovers and temporary amnesia. Well, things have changed dramatically, as this book shows. New equipment and new ingredients have altered everything. Nowadays you don't need a Degree in Science, or to risk divorce. The Great Australian Home-Brew Book shows you that making beer is as easy as making a cup of coffee.

For people who enjoy drinking, rather than making, we tell you how to get the very best from a brewing can with an absolute minimum of fuss. For people who get particular satisfaction from making beer, we include more craft information and a collection of recipes, using the talents of local brewers. Importantly, all the equipment and ingredients described in the book are available locally. It is also good to know that in a world of additives, preservatives colourings and chemicals, the beer you brew is under your control.

Well, now is the time to get going, so you can enjoy drinking your own in just a few weeks time.

1 WHERE *to start...*

There is nothing particularly magical about making your own beer. But the result is like magic. In a matter of a few weeks you have a perfectly enjoyable brew. A crisp, clear beer that is great value for money. You can choose home-brew cans in 1.5 kg or 1.8 kg sizes. These have everything ready, the hops, malted barley, even a yeast sachet. All you need is water and sugar, to make around 20 litres of beer. That is equal to about 5 dozen tinnies, or more accurately about 2½ dozen 750ml or quart bottles. One of the reasons you will be amazed at the low per-bottle-cost of your home-brew is that you are not paying excise tax.

There is a choice of over 250 different brands and styles of home-brew cans on the shelves of home-brew shops – even supermarkets stock a limited range. You can brew everything from Canadian, Scottish, English, American and Australian beers – lagers, draughts, bitters, stouts, super-strength, milds – you name it and you'll probably find a can for it. That is why the search for just the right taste is a pleasure.

Most home-brew shops have beer tasting where you can try a glass of a new beer or an established favourite. Even an absolute beginner is virtually guaranteed a successful beer first time. Your home-brew shop will be more than happy to answer any queries, even over the phone.

One thing to remember is that by law you can brew as much beer as you like but you must not sell any, whatsoever. That includes making donations of bottles to school fairs or for raffle prizes.

One of the most important skills a home-brewer must have is the ability to boast about the quality of his beer, tell outrageous lies about his special never-to-be revealed technique, and a dedication to quality control. Quality control demands constant sampling of every finished brew, right to the last drop, just to make sure each and every bottle is just as good as the last. We recommend that these tests should be carried out on a regular basis.

2 BASIC *equipment...*

When it comes to equipment it is unwise to stint. The items you need have no moving parts and will last for countless brews. Some old books talk about making your own equipment with jam jars, using oaken casks, rubbish bins and rubber hoses. Forget that. We live in the plastic age and plastic is best for brewing. The savings you make on the first couple of brews will more than pay for the best equipment. Many brew shops sell complete starter kits with all the basics. You can, however, build your equipment item by item from brew shops, hardware shops or supermarkets.

Here's what you need to begin

25-litre barrel or bucket with an airtight lid. This should be of food-grade polythene. A bung near the base will allow for a tap to be fitted to make bottle filling easier. The big wide lid will make it easier to clean. Heavy-grade plastic brew bags are also on sale at home brew shops.

Airlock and bung for the top of your fermenting barrel. This allows the carbon dioxide gas to escape during fermentation and protects the beer from airborne bacteria and the dreaded fruitfly which will ruin your brew.

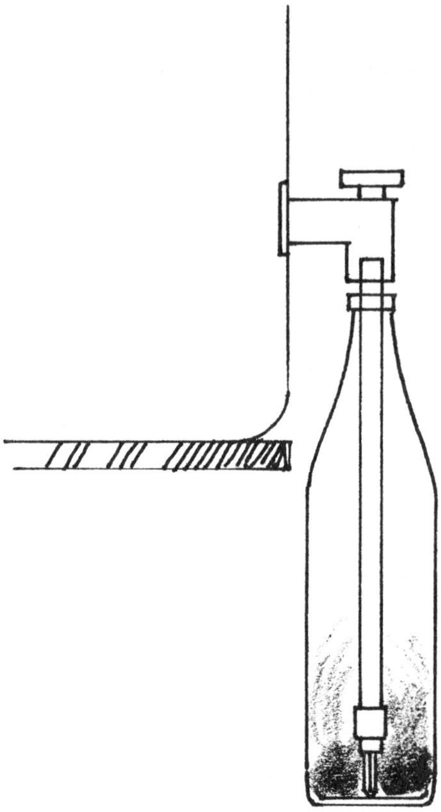

Brewer's Tap

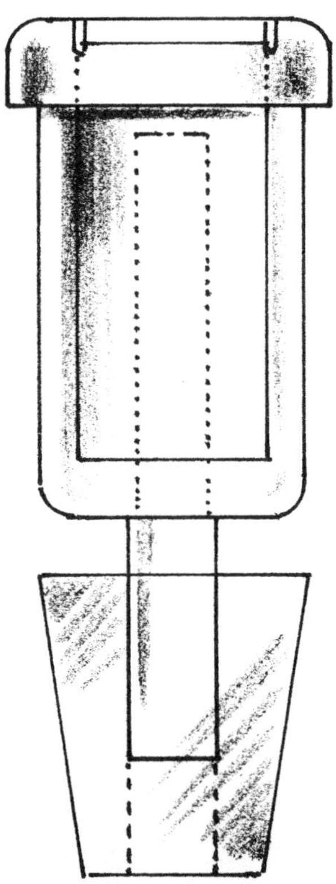

Airlock-type 'A'

Brewers tap which fits the base tap. This makes bottle filling simple, with minimum disturbance of the deposit at the bottom of the barrel. This device is cheap and easy to use with two great advantages. It is easier to use and control than the siphon tube, and operates when the bottle base is pushed against the base of the tap as the illustration shows. The more difficult, but just as reliable way, is the clear siphon tube. You will need about 1.5 metres of tube. Use it carefully because you do not want to siphon up any of the deposit on the bottom of your barrel.

A simple clothes peg will serve to control the depth of the tube inside your barrel. Gradually ease the tube into the barrel clipping the clothes peg on the tube as you go. This will not close the tube but it will give you some idea of how deep in to the barrel your tube has gone. This is important because you want to avoid sucking up the sediment and adding oxygen to your beer. The more disturbed your beer becomes the more you allow oxygen to mix with your beer increasing the possibilities of contamination.

Hydrometer. This sounds very scientific but it is no more difficult to read that a thermometer. We will tell you more about this in another chapter. Essentially, the hydrometer tells you when to bottle, and how things are progressing. It is not very expensive and will possibly save you cleaning up exploding bottles.

Long Plastic Spoon. Most home-brewers steal this item from the kitchen. If there is no plastic, wood is okay. Salad servers, parfait spoons, in fact any unused wedding presents or similar, if not made of metal, will do.

Bottle Caps. These can be bought in bulk from supermarkets and brew shops. The caps with the plastic seal are the cheapest and the best.

Large Pot. This is also traditionally stolen from the kitchen. Almost any pot that will take 4 litres of water (about 5 beer bottles) will be okay. The lid is optional because we're only using it to boil water.

Empty Bottles. These must be standard 750 ml or 355 ml glass bottles, the kind that are sold in crates or cartons. The CO2 build-up, or pressure, in a beer bottle is greater than the P.S.I. you have in your car tyre. That is why it is vital that you only use glass that can withstand pressure. Any non-returnable or one-trip glass bottle could explode. In an emergency brown Pet soft drink bottles can be used, resealing with the original cap, but they are not as good and tend to taint the beer. Avoid them if you can.

Airlock-type 'B'

3 WHAT MAKES *a beer?*

Basically your beer consists of only 5 ingredients.
MALT. This gives your beer flavour, strength and the distinctive aroma.
HOPS. These add the bitterness to balance the maltiness.
SUGAR OR DEXTROSE. This gives the strength and sweetness.
YEAST. This is a living thing that converts the sugar into alcohol and carbon dioxide gas.
WATER. Even the strongest beers are over 90% water. Don't bother to impart this little gem of knowledge to your mates in the pub. They probably won't appreciate being reminded how expensive that water is when it's sold over the bar!

4 WHAT GOES ON IN THE *barrel...*

When you put yeast into a sugary solution it begins to multiply with great speed, quickly forming millions of yeast cells. The alcohol we are after is a by-product of this reproduction process.

The airlock is used to cut off the yeast's air supply and forces the yeast into a secondary method of reproduction, which it can do without oxygen. This results in more alcohol and that's good news because that is what makes our beer different from ginger beer. For the kit-beer home-brewer there is a great debate between sugar and Dextrose. Well, here are the pros and cons so you can decide for yourself.

Dextrose is an "invert sugar". It is marginally more expensive and brews out faster than cane sugar. Dextrose eliminates one stage in the process of converting sugar to alcohol. It also creates less sediment. This sediment is firmer and more compact too and so is less likely to be disturbed in the bottling process. Apart from these practical advantages many experienced brewers use nothing else as they maintain it produces a better beer with better head retention and gas retention.

Ordinary white sugar is easier to find, less expensive and brews about the same amount of alcohol. Weight for weight, Dextrose and sugar can be substituted for each other in equal quantities.

Dextrose is used by commercial breweries. If you are driving for a consistent quality of brew we believe Dextrose to be worth the extra cents.

5 CLEAN EQUIPMENT MAKES A *fail safe brew!*

Hygiene for home-brewers is the most important step of all. The whole process of brewing is creating a sugary, warm liquid that sits around for some time. This creates the perfect climate for everything you don't want, like bacteria, mould, wild yeasts, flies and who knows what else, to wreck all your good work and your brew!

When we say clean everything we mean everything. Now this is not as difficult as it sounds. Sodium Metabisulphite, when mixed with water, creates sulphur dioxide which is used commercially in the meat and fruit industry to kill all known germs. Best of all it is very economical, efficient and easy to buy. Sodium Metabisulphite has no effect whatsoever on equipment, is totally biodegradable and is destroyed on contact with oxygen. To give you some idea of its safety, wine makers routinely add Sodium Metabisulphite to their wines several times during making because it only reacts with oxygen and is untraceable in the finished wine.

There are a few words of warning, however. The same fumes that sterilize everything for you can cause discomfort if breathed deeply by people with breathing difficulties. Make sure there is air circulation in enclosed spaces and there should be no problem. In fact SO2 is the only permitted preservative allowed in commercial beer.

The easiest way to use Sulphur Metabisulphite is to use a stock solution for even more economy. Mix

50 g (3 level Tbsp) in 1 litre of warm water. This creates a 5% strength solution by weight of available sulphur dioxide. This will keep up to 5 months in a tightly sealed bottle.

For cleaning you need only a 1 - 2% solution. So when using, use 1 part of your stock solution to 5 parts of water. This creates a normal sterilizing strength ideal for purifying bottles, barrels, siphon tubes and all your other equipment. If you put all the equipment in your barrel, swish it around and leave for about one hour so everything will be sterile. Small items like hydrometers can be safely left in the solution to keep them sterile. If you are not using your barrel for some time, add a little of your concentrated solution to the barrel, seal it, and it will stay clean and sweet smelling.

Talking about your fermenting barrel – every four or five brews give it a really thorough treatment to remove any taint from previous brews that may have been slightly absorbed by the plastic. This is also a great opportunity to give everything else the treatment by putting all your brewing equipment in the barrel. Fill your 5 gallon fermenter to the top with cold water and add 50 ml (3 Tbsp) of ordinary household bleach. You can steal this from the laundry – it will be called Chlorine bleach, Chlorogene or similar. Give it a stir and leave over night. Next day rinse with warm or hot water. Then put in 4 tsp of Sodium Metabisulphite and 250 ml of warm water and swish it over all surfaces, put the sealed lid back on and it will keep the container fresh and sterile until your next brew.

Be sure to rinse all Sodium Metabisulphite from all surfaces that come into contact with your beer for it inhibits yeast and may make your brew "stick".

Your fermenting barrel should be washed out immediately after use to remove the "lees" or dead yeast deposit. Otherwise this may encourage mould growths and any on the sides can cake and become difficult to remove.

Bottle cleaning is undoubtedly the most boring of all the home-brewer's jobs. However, it must be done and done well. Just remember every bottle you clean is going to be emptied later into your glass. The first time you brew you will probably have assembled a collection of bottles, preferably complete with crates. You will need at least 30 bottles to be on the safe side.

If you can, swap these for freshly emptied bottles from a party or social club while the dregs are still liquid as they will be easier to clean. If you have been lucky or have purchased new plastic bottles, proceed with the normal system described in the next paragraph.

If you have got a bottle collection of unknown age and origin, here is what to do. Buy a bottle brush and Chempro or CXA sterilizer and cleaner. Mix these according to directions and fill each bottle and allow to soak. Now get to work with the bottle brush. These chemicals should make any deposits easy to move and most should float to the surface without any brushing. Now put your bottle brush away because if you follow the system we're about to describe you should never have to use it again. With freshly used home-brew bottles, rinse immediately with hot water. Hold the bottles up to the light and when sediment-free, store upside down in a crate. This keeps the bottles nice and clean. When you are ready to bottle it is comparatively simple to give each bottle a rinse with hot water to remove any dust.

Use your stock Sodium Metabisulphite diluted 5 to 1 in a jug and with a funnel (yes it's back to "borrow from the kitchen" again) pour the solution from bottle to bottle. Allow to stand for about half and hour, then rinse again to remove the Sodium Metabisulphite. Now you are ready to bottle with clean bottles.

As a general rule make sure that everything that comes into contact with your beer is clean and sterile and you will never lose a brew or even a single bottle. A word of caution. Do not tell anybody about your sudden interest in cleanliness and hygiene as this could accidently involve you in extra tasks around the place that could waste valuable "quality control" time!

6 YEAST - *Nature's Magic!*

Yeast is a living thing. It is in the air about us, even on your skin. When yeast is deprived of moisture it forms spores and that is what is in the "dried yeast" pack in your home-brew kit.

There is one major difference between the strains of wild yeast and the yeast in your kit and it all comes down to the particular strain used by the maker of your kit. No two yeasts are exactly the same. They work at different speeds and have a significant effect on the final taste of your beer. One of the important reasons for hygiene is that we must kill the wild yeasts until the beer yeast takes control.

Temperatures over 35 degrees Centigrade will kill yeast. At temperatures below 10 degrees it becomes dormant and the brew will tend to "stick". The ideal temperature for yeast is in the 18 to 24°C range. Colder and the yeast will work erratically. Warmer and the yeast may bubble away the aroma and damage the head of beer in the barrel. All this tender loving care with the yeast is worth it. Every bubble of C02 it produces through your airlock means an equal weight of alcohol created in the barrel.

Temperatures

Yeast works best in a constant temperature. Not too hot one hour and too cold the next. Your 25 litre barrel helps moderate temperatures and the yeast itself creates a few degrees of heat as it is working. Winter can pose a problem, however.

There are some simple answers. The hot water cupboard can be requisitioned if there is enough headroom, the temperature is about right and the towels won't notice the difference. If this minor reorganization of the house creates problems with

MAKE YOUR OWN HEATING BOX...

1. UPTURNED TEA CHEST
2. 100 WATT HANDY LAMP
3. 3 CORE FLEX
4. LIGHT DIMMER SWITCH
5. 3 PIN PLUG
6. CORK WITH HOLE
7. THERMOMETER
8. FERMENTING BIN
9. INSPECTION DOOR
10. NEWSPAPER OR CARD UNDER BOX AS INSULATION

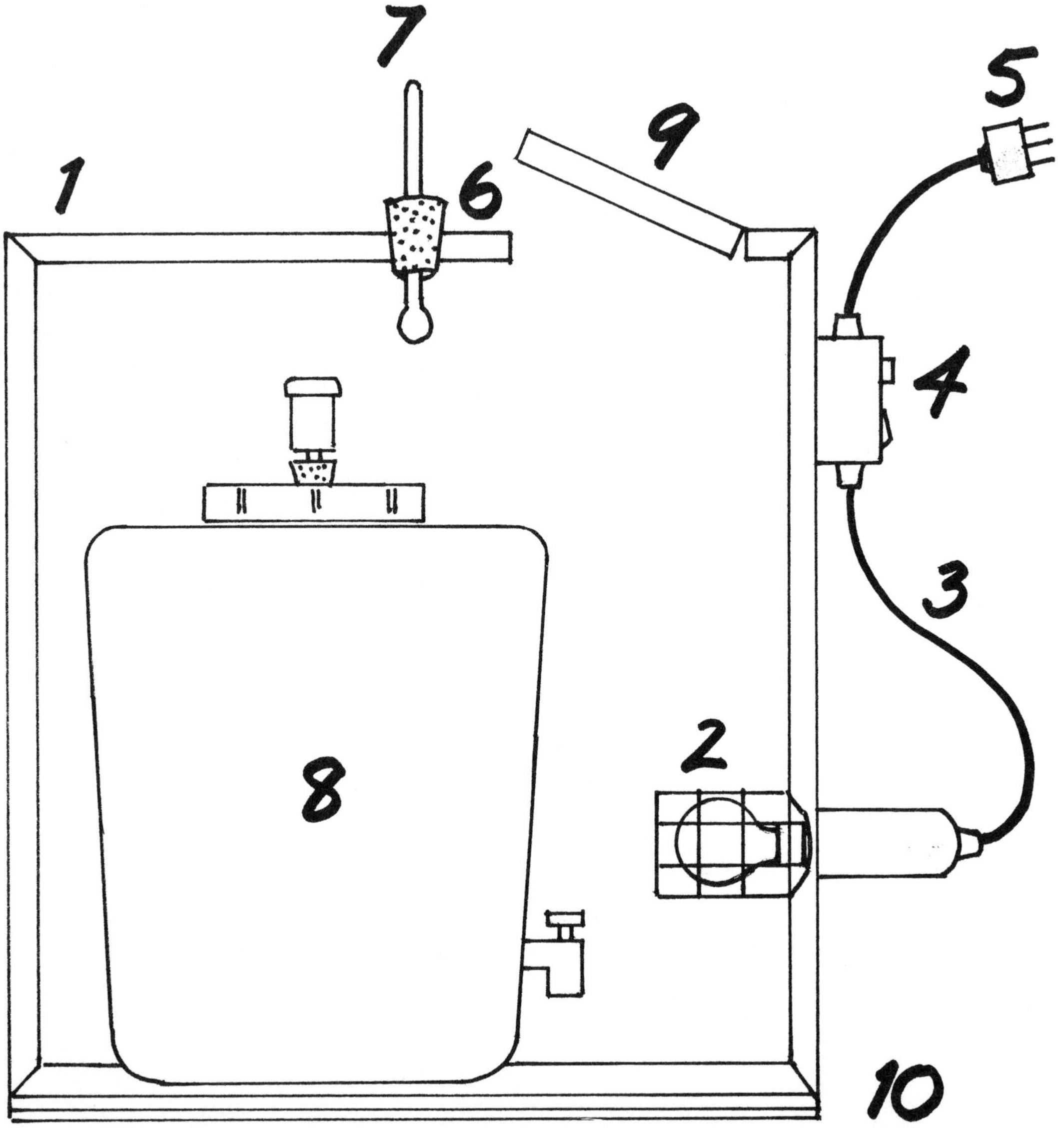

hard-hearted members of the household who do not share your concern with the happiness of yeast, consider the possibility of a tea chest or heated cabinet. Bore a hole in the bottom side of the cabinet or chest, install a socket and fit a 60 watt lightbulb. Cover the top with a few layers of old fabric and this will trap and warm the air to the right temperature.

Other possibilities for creating warmth are the brew-belt, or a heated pad, available from home-brew shops. The brew-belt sits around the outside of the barrel like a lasso and temperatures can be adjusted by moving the belt up and down the barrel. The heated pad sits under the barrel and gives a constant heat. Both are completely sealed, waterproof and cannot overheat because the temperature is controlled by the size of the heating cable. They have no thermostat or other fiddly bits to break or fail. Theoretically they should last a lifetime. Perhaps their best feature is that they never need come into contact with your brew so there's no chance of contamination. They do not have to be constantly checked, adjusted or cleaned. They cost about the same as a weak lightbulb to run and require less attention.

Beware of immersion heaters and leftovers from aquariums. They are awkward to fit and make airtight. Because they come directly into contact with the brew they need to be cleaned. Adjustment can also be difficult and could cost you a few experimental brews.

On average your brew kit beer will take from six to ten days to work out at the ideal temperature. Do not be worried if it takes a little longer. Remember, a slow constant brew makes a better brew.

If you are using any heating method, give your beer a cold break two days before bottling. This helps settle the sediment stirred up by heat convection in the barrel and gives you a clearer brew.

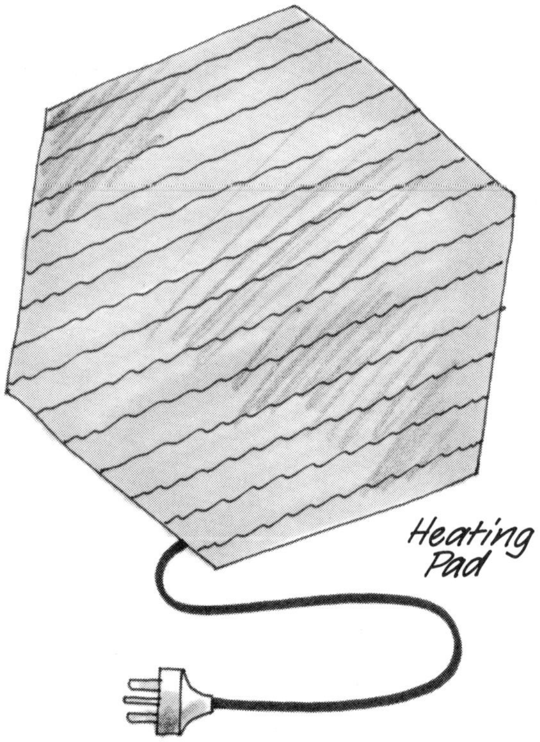

7 BOTTLING

Remember use only returnable bottles. Bottle as soon as convenient after your brew has stopped working. This stops your beer absorbing off-flavours from the dead yeast left on the bottom of the barrel. Make sure your bottles are sterile, primed with 1 level tsp (10 ml spoon) of sugar for 750 ml bottles to create the fizz and head. Use ½ level tsp for smaller bottles. Fill to about 1 inch or 3 cm from the top with beer, then cap.

First, leave the bottles in a warm place for two days. Then move them to a cooler place to mature.

Now comes the hard part – the wait. Your beer will be drinkable after about two weeks. If you can control your pouring aim for longer, your brew will get better after recovering from the shock of bottling. The priming too will work better developing a better head. Three months is the ideal maturing time for your home-brew.

8 HOW TO USE YOUR *hydrometer . . .*

A hydrometer is one of the best investments you can make. It tells you how much sugar to add to get the alcohol level you want. You can also check the

progress of your brew and make sure it is still working. Most importantly the hydrometer tells you when it is bottling time. That means you can eliminate all the problems of exploding bottles.

Basically your hydrometer is a weighted glass tube that is calibrated down the side from 1.000 or less on the top to about 1.120 on the bottom. It is calibrated to float in pure water at 1.000 – this is the S.G. or specific gravity of water. Sugar or Dextrose makes the water thicker and the hydrometer will not sink so far; as the yeast converts this sugar into alcohol the hydrometer sinks further and further into the brew.

In beer making the starting S.G. varies from 1.035 for light beers to 1.060 for strong beers. Fill a trial jar (or any clear jar longer than your hydrometer) and test your Opening Gravity – a brew kit will recommend how much sugar or Dextrose to add so this step is unnecessary but interesting. This reading can be used to give a potential alcohol figure.

S.G. Reading	Potential % alcohol by volume
1.010	.9
1.015	1.6
1.020	2.3
1.025	3.0
1.030	3.7
1.035	4.4
1.040	5.1
1.045	5.8
1.050	6.5
1.055	7.2
1.060	7.8

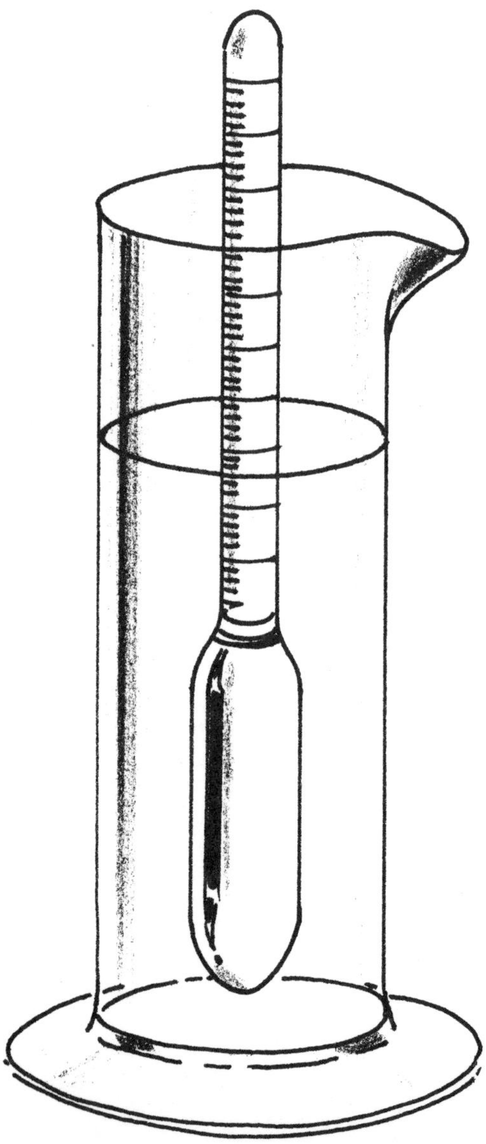

Most recipes will give a recommended addition of sugar but if you want to adjust the alcohol content remember 56 g (2¼ oz) of sugar per 4.5 litres (1 gallon) will raise the S.G. reading by 5 degrees of gravity.

After fermentation has finished, or if you think it has finished, check the S.G. with your hydrometer. If it reads about 1.008 or less it is safe to bottle. Never bottle above 1.010. Your hydrometer is probably calibrated to be accurate at 15°C, but small temperature variations are relatively insignificant. For example at 11°C you should subtract 0.6 and at 27°C add 2.0.

Surface tension also affects the way you should read an hydrometer. Surface tension curves the surface of the liquid and causes a slightly false reading. Always read your hydrometer at eye level. As you can see from the illustration on page 25, the reading can be deceptive as the liquid is higher at the point the liquid meets the surface of the hydrometer and the trial jar.

9 MAKING BETTER BEER

with a brew kit can.

1) Remove all persons, dogs, etc from kitchen.
2) Read the instructions. They vary.
3) Put the can in hot water for five minutes or more. (The water can be very hot, but not boiling.) This helps make the contents of the can easier to pour.
4) Bring to the boil about 4.5 litres of water (1 gallon).
5) Check the drainage tap is closed then pour the content of your can into the clean and sterilized fermenting bin.
6) Add 1 kg of Dextrose Monohydrate or 1 kg sugar.
7) Add the 4.5 litres of boiling water and stir thoroughly.
8) Rinse can with extra boiling/hot water – about 500 ml – and add to fermenter. This is to get the last of the contents into your brew.
9) Top up with cold water to fill fermenter.
10) You may have to let the fermenter stand covered – until the temperature reaches 18 - 21°C (65 - 70°F) – the ideal brewing temperature – before you add your yeast from the sachet. However, if you use only 3 litres of boiling water in the first instance (step 4 above) the water will be almost exactly the right temperature to pitch your yeast immediately.
11) Clean up kitchen – there is hardly any mess, just empty water pots to dry. Then allow the rightful owner of kitchen to return.
12) Wait and watch your airlock for anything from one week to one month until bubbles stop.
13) Check with hydrometer and bottle when ready.
14) Enjoy!

10 TRICKS OF THE TRADE

to improve your brew.

1) Store your beer in the dark – sunlight affects the colour and flavour.
2) If you are using any heat source, give your beer in the fermenter a cold break for about 24 hours before bottling. This will help settle the sediment.
3) Your fermenter lid should be airtight so that a squeeze will move the airlock water. Do not damage it with over-tightening. The CO_2 layer produced by fermentation automatically creates a protective layer over your beer. Remember you're not taking your fermenter into outer space.
4) A slow fermentation will give you a better-tasting beer with a better head.
5) When serving, pour your beer from bottles into a jug, leaving the sediment behind in the bottles. Then pour it into your glass.
6) Put Sodium Metabisulphite in your airlock as it will help kill bacteria.
7) Do not fill your fermenter right to the top when you first add cold water, leave head room for another 4 litres. Your yeast will begin with a hiss and a roar and beer may overflow through your airlock in the first few days. The extra space you leave will stop this problem. Top up with water after 3-4 days while brew is still quite active.
8) Keep all metal away from your beer. Use plastic wherever possible or stainless steel. Contact with metal quickly gives your beer a metallic taste.

11 MAKING YOUR OWN BEER

from square one!

Making your own beer can be as complicated or as simple as you like. You can begin by growing your own hops and barley or starting anywhere further along the path. In this book we have attempted to keep the method as straightforward as possible and make the beers as good as possible. To do this we have followed the steps of the great commercial brewers and adapted them for your kitchen.

Beer making is a natural process. We do not really make beer. Beer makes itself. All we do is prepare the way and enjoy the results.

Here is what goes into your beer and why. The malt gives your beer body and flavour. The hops add flavour "tang" and bitterness. Sugar provides the alcohol and some residual sweetness. Yeast converts this sugar into alcohol and the water creates 90% of the volume of your beer. There are also a number of minor ingredients, which will be explained later, and these all help in the beer-making process.

EQUIPMENT YOU WILL NEED FOR 20 LITRES OF BEER

Do not rush out and buy a vast amount of equipment before you make at least a couple of experimental brews. Then you will discover just what you really need and what kind and size etc., of equipment will best suit your brewing methods. Here is a basic list – if you are already a kit brewer you may have most of this equipment on hand.

- A Large Pot – (or thermostatically controlled boiler). The pot should be stainless steel and able to hold 10 litres (2.0 gallons) – a lid is not essential.
- 1 25-litre plastic fermenting bin with lid and tap.
- 1 20-litre plastic bucket with lid.
- Large plastic spoon for stirring brew.
- Hydrometer and jar.
- Kitchen scales.
- Large sieve/muslin bar or brewing bag.
- Small funnel.
- Kitchen measuring spoons.
- 1.5 metres of plastic siphon tube.
- Bottlebrush.
- Thermometer (0-100°C).

BASIC INGREDIENTS

While this is not an exhaustive list, it will give you some idea of how uncomplicated home-brewing can be and is sufficient to get you brewing. A more detailed explanation of ingredients appears in the next chapter.

You will need:

- Irish moss.
- Beer nutrient salts.
- Sugar.
- Hops – you store these in the fridge.
- Malt extract.
- Yeast sachets – also store in the fridge.
- Crushed crystal malt.
- Flaked barley.
- And don't forget your Sodium Metabisulphite for hygiene.
- Make sure everything you use is sterile.

12 THE INGREDIENTS *and what they do...*

Your first visit to a home-brew shop can be a rather daunting experience with what seems to be a vast array of ingredients, chemicals, acids and grains usually with very little label explanation. Here is what they would tell you if they had the space on the label.

Pale malt grains. In making beer yeast ferments a sugary solution called the wort. Most of this wort consists of barley grains that have been altered by you by "mashing", described in the next chapter, or by a commercial malt maker to extract the maltose from the malt. Crushed pale malt allows the maximum of this maltose to be extracted. This is the main ingredient of your beer.

Lager malt grains. This looks very similar to Pale malt even though it has been more lightly roasted. Yes, the grains are larger.

Roasted grains. These colour and flavour your beer. The great range of these reflects the hundreds of different beers that are brewed in the world. They only represent a small proportion of the total amount of malt you use but make a disproportionate amount of difference to your final beer. They range from Crystal malt, Amber malt, Brown malt, Chocolate malt, Roast barley to Patent black malt.

Malt extracts. When we get to the chapter on "Brewing Method" you will see just how much work has been done for you. The "mashing" has already been done and the results concentrated to just 10% of the original volume.

Flaked rice. This is just squashed rice and is used as a substitute and addition for malt and has very little flavour.

Flaked barley. This helps hold the head on your beer and adds body and flavour.

Hops. You can just about taste the names – Sticklebract, Super Alpha, even Pride of Ringwood. There are a whole range of hops, each suitable for a certain kind of beer style. The essential oils and resins of hops give beer its bitterness and aroma, to balance the sweetness of the malt. They are the dried female flowers of the hop vine and they make beer, beer.
There are many varieties of hops you can buy for home brewing. They come in many forms, such as pelletts, dried flowers, and extracts. If the hops we mention here are unavailable, simply ask your brew shop for advice on what the best substitution would be. All hops have different flavours, so feel free to experiment and create your own original brew.

Sugar. These recipes suggest a combination of sugars like dark sugars, white sugars, caster sugars, Dextrose monohydrate and glucose chips. These add character to beers. Making substitutions will change your beer. Fortunately all sugar is not too expensive and is easy to store and to buy.

Water. Boil as much of the water as you can for use in your beer. If you have access to rainwater or spring water, lucky you! Your tap water will do but may need treatment to adjust for the minute quantities of dissolved mineral salts that can affect your beer. Here is how to get the right water for your beer. The figures give treatment for water in 25 litre (5 gallon) lots.

Type of beer	Hard water	Soft water
Lager	A	
Light ale } Bitter ale} Pale ale }	A&B	B
Brown ale } Mild ale } Mild stout}	A&C	C
Dry stout		D

(A) Add 5 ml (1 tsp) Calcium chloride or Lactic acid.
(B) Add 5 ml Gypsum (Calcium sulphate) and 2.5 ml Epsom salts.
(C) Add 2.5 ml plain salt.
(D) Add 5 ml chalk (Calcium carbonate).

Yeast. Yeast creates the alcohol and plays an important part in the flavour of beer. Buy only good quality yeasts and only beer yeasts. Do not wreck a brew by saving a few cents. Always re-hydrate yeasts before you use them. A clean glass with warm water will reactivate the yeast faster. A starter bottle is even better. It gives the yeast time to establish a viable colony so your brew will be up and working faster. This also lessens the chances of a wild yeast establishing itself.

13 RECIPE FOR *a starter bottle.*

(Make up at least 24 hours before pitching yeast).

Boil 500 ml of water and pour into sterilized bottle. Dissolve 8 g (one dessert spoon) of sugar, add 4 g (one tsp) yeast nutrient, and dissolve. Plug with cotton wool. When mixture is below 30°C add one tsp (level) of your chosen yeast. Plug again with cotton wool, give it a swirl and leave in a warm place.

Yeast nutrients. These help get yeast actively multiplying and help stop fermentations sticking. Use a ready made up pack from a brew shop or use this recipe to make your own.

Citric acid	50%	30 g (2 Tbsp)
Ammonium phosphate	35%	20 g (1½ Tbsp)
Sulphate of magnesium (Epsom salts)	15%	8 g (2 tsp)
Common salt	5%	4 g (1 tsp)

Exact measures are not important but keep to rough proportions. Add 2 level tsp of this well mixed plus ½ cup of strong tea per 20 litres.

Like you, yeast needs food to be at its best. The acid helps aid fermentation. Even 1 tsp of Citric acid alone will help. The tannin in the cold tea will help if you use finings. In an emergency, for instance, if your bottled stock is reaching dangerously low levels, then 1/2 a tsp of Marmite or Vegemite added to the mixture will save the day.

Other extras.

Caramel – is basically burned sugar and adds colour to your beer.

Torrified barley – this barley has popped like popcorn.

Isomerised hop extracts – these processed extracts of hop bitter resins can be added after your beer has finished fermenting, to make final adjustments to the bitterness. They are not as good as real hops, so be careful of shortcuts.

Irish moss – is not a moss at all. It is a kind of seaweed that helps clear the beer by making the solids (the cloudy particles) settle on the bottom of the fermenter.

Brewers Finings – the most popular way to clear beer. Many brands are sold and all work like Irish moss. Used as directed they can clear even the most cloudy beers.

Gelatine – a common ingredient of branded fining products, gelatine can be used alone to achieve the same clarity in beer. 15 g (1 Tbsp) of gelatine dissolved in a little warm beer will clear 20 litres.

Lactose – a milk sugar used for sweetening. This sugar cannot ferment so will not be converted to alcohol by the yeast. It creates a residual sweetness if your beer is too bitter.

Licorice – adds colour to beer.

LET'S GET BREWING.

Now we come to the second most enjoyable task of the home-brewer, making the beer. (Drinking your beer is the most enjoyable part.) Here you will find a whole new language which is explained as we go. You will discover new phrases such as "sparging your wort", which sounds like something you should do in private, but you will soon get the hang of it. Our recipes use malted barley and malt extract so we will explain both methods. Some recipes include a little of both procedures so it is best to understand both. We have tried to keep the procedures as simple as possible and within the capabilities of the average kitchen.

Home-brewing using malt extract from the can.

Remember, using malt extract means much of the

work has been done for us so we are in effect beginning half-way through the brewing process.

Stage 1 – Boiling.
Heat up about 15 litres of hot water in your large saucepan. Before the water boils add your can of malt extract and dissolve this mixture completely before adding more heat to bring mixture to the boil. When boiling add half the amount of hops in the recipe. Boil for 1 hour. After 1 hour add a quarter of the hops and keep boiling; these hops add flavour. In the last half-hour of the boil (total boil time 1½ hours) add the final quarter of the hops and all the Irish moss in the last 15 minutes. These hops add aroma. The first few minutes of the boil will create much frothing and bubbling so keep your eye out for overflows. Turn down the heat to a quieter boil if necessary. The resulting liquid is called the wort.

Stage II – Strain off. Use a large sieve, muslin cloth or the grain bag (described in the next section) and strain this wort into your fermenting bin. Pour a jug-full of hot water into your sieve or cloth to get the most of the hop extract and add this to your fermenting bin. Throw away the hops.

Stage III – Add the sugar.
Dissolve all the sugars used in a pot of hot water and add this to your fermenter. Add any sweeteners like Lactose, Saccharin or any artificial sweeteners at this stage.

Stage IV – Top up.
Add cold water (boiled and allowed to cool preferably), to bring your fermenter up to the 20 litre mark.

Stage V – Use your hydrometer.
When your 20 litres of wort has cooled to room temperature, check with your hydrometer to see if you have reached your "Original Gravity" or O.G. in the recipe. If not add extra fermentable sugar at the rate described in the hydrometer chapter.

Stage VI – Primary fermentation.
After your wort has reached the room temperature (ideally 18°C - 21°C) pitch your yeast. Fit the lid and the beer will start working. Keep the beer well protected until it is working

well and produces its own protective blanket of CO_2.

Use an airlock if you have plenty of head-room in your fermenter. Your beer should now be bubbling underneath an unwanted layer of foamy scum. Skim off this scum and give the beer a good stir with your plastic spoon. After three days things will begin to die down.

Stage VII – Secondary fermentation.
Siphon your beer into your final fermenter. This leaves a layer of yeast and debris at the bottom of the initial bucket, and helps stop "off-flavours" developing. Fit the airlock and wait until beer stops working. Check with hydrometer.

Stage VIII – Beer at last.
Wait 24 to 48 hours before you bottle or cask. Some brewers automatically add gelatine before secondary fermentation to clear all their beers.

HOME BREWING USING MALTED GRAIN.

Here's your chance to become the Master Brewer and this is where you get to "sparge your wort" in the privacy of your kitchen.

Stage 1 – Mashing. This is a natural process that allows water to break down the starches in the cracked grain into fermentable sugars. This breakdown is caused by the enzyme diastase. Temperatures are very important to allow this enzyme to work.

There is a choice of mashing systems here. Your method will probably depend on the household budget. In both cases mix dry grains and cereals together by hand then mix them again to make a porridge mash.

SYSTEM-A: Using your large boiling pan.
Every 1 kg of mixed grain and cereal needs 3 - 5 litres of water. Some recipes use up to 5 kg of this "grist". You need a rather large pan for both this and the boiling stage.

First pour water into pan and heat to 60°C. Gradually stir in the grist, avoiding lumps, until it becomes a smooth porridge. Continue stirring and slowly raise the temperature to 67°C. Switch off the heat. Then stir and bring back up to this heat. Try to maintain temperature for 1½ hours in the 65°C - 67°C range. You may have

SPARGING
EXTRACTING THE GOODNESS FROM BARLEY MALT.
WASH THE GRAIN GENTLY WITH HOT WATER...
MASHED MALT HELD IN A GRAIN BAG SIEVE SUPPORTED IN A POLYETHYLENE BUCKET...
BOILER

to reheat a couple of times. Do not forget to stir while reheating.

SYSTEM B: Brew boiler. Use the same initial procedure to reach 67 °C then set the dial and stir occasionally. Ideally, have the grain in a grain bag so you can carry on the next stage leaving the bulk of the wort in the boiler. Remember this bag may have to hold 5 kg so it must be strong.

STAGE II – Sparging your wort. Now all is revealed. This is the process of finally extracting the malt sugars from the grain. Much of this valuable sugar is trapped by the grain and needs to be released. Support the grain bag in a polythene bucket, or make a sieve of nylon netting or similar and suspend this above a bucket. Let the grains drain naturally. Capture the first litre or so in a beer jug and pour back over the grain. When the grain is reasonably dry, gently pour hot water over the grain until you have your 20 litres of wort.

Stage III. Continue with boiling as described in Stage I in the Malt extract procedure (see p. 36) and continue through to Stage VIII.

METHODS OF MASHING

1 USING A BOILING PAN OR DIXIE

MIX THE CRUSHED MALT GRAINS WITH HOT WATER IN A BOILING PAN AND KEEP TEMPERATURE CLOSE TO 66°C (150°F) FOR 1½ HOURS.

NORMAL TEMPERATURE RANGE

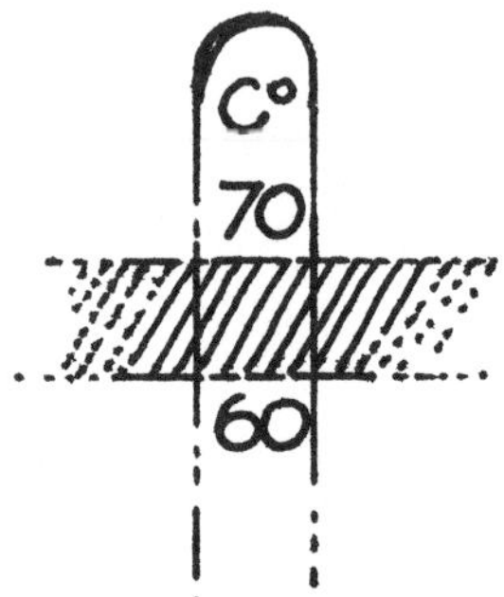

2 USING A BREWING BOILER

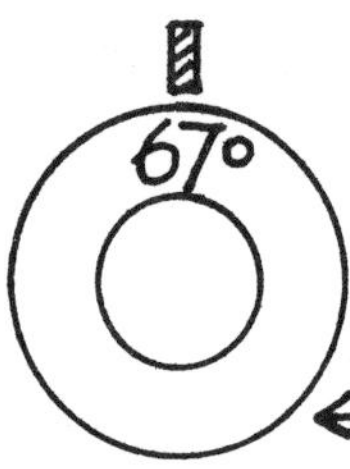

SET DIAL ON BOILER TO GIVE CORRECT TEMPERATURE.

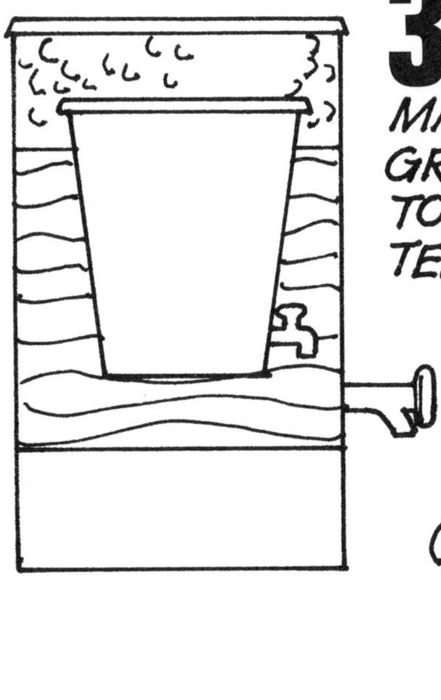

3 FLOATING MASH TON

MASHING BUCKET CONTAINING GRAIN, FLOATED IN HOT WATER TO ENSURE AN EVEN TEMPERATURE AROUND 66° C.

A SUCCESSFUL MASH...

A DROP OF IODINE ADDED TO A SAMPLE OF THE MASHED GRAIN SHOULD NOT CHANGE COLOUR (TO BLUISH BLACK) WHEN MASHING IS COMPLETED.

WHAT TO DO WHEN THINGS GO WRONG

Things do go wrong, even for the most experienced brewer. Some problems can be fixed but unfortunately if a beer goes wrong it is usually "down the drain".

Common problems are:

Stuck fermentation – S.G. will not go down and the beer stops working. This could be caused by -
a) Temperature too low – move your beer to a warmer place. It should start working again.
b) Inadequate nutrients - add 2.5ml (½ tsp) of citric acid per 5 litres.
c) Lack of oxygen – pour the beer into a bucket and back into your fermenter from a height and stir.

No fermentation – the yeast may have been killed before use – buy a new yeast and use a starter bottle.

Acetification – beer has vinegary smell. Beer can be attacked by the vinegar baccillus Mycoderma aceti. This lives in the air and is commonly transported to beer by the vinegar fly. There is not much to do except pretend you wanted to make vinegar all along! Add another 500 g of sugar per 5 litres and allow to ferment out to get an excellent malt vinegar.

HANDY HINTS

The cooler the temperature the beer works at the better the beer. Lager should have an even lower temperature – 12°C to 14°C is ideal.

100 g of crushed crystal malt or grain = 1 cup.
30 g of loose hops = 1 cup.

Travelling with beer – chill beer for 24 hours and siphon into P.E.T. bottle.

Special competition siphons are sold at brew shops – they leave the sediment and transfer only the beer.

Do not boil any grain – try the lazy method instead. Boil 2 litres of water, take off heat, add grains, stir and leave to cool.

Hops should be kept in a freezer or fridge.

Allow a cold break between the first and second fermentation, and before you bottle or cask.

EXTRA GOODIES YOU CAN BUY

Brew shops are really toy shops for grown-ups. And they are just as much fun. Here are some of the more exotic labour savers available.

Water filters – to remove chlorine and all the chemical "nasties" that affect your beer.
Bottle washers – fit to the top of your tap and clean your bottles with tiny ball bearings.
Nylon brew bags – for hop bars and sparging – never wash muslin again.
Siphon 'u' bends – fit on end of siphon tube and pull liquid down your fermenter, not up from the bottom, so sediment is undisturbed.
Self-heated thermostatically-controlled boilers – take all the guesswork out of temperature control.
Pressure casks – they hold an entire finished brew and take all the bottle-washing work from your shoulders. Now you have endless beer at your elbow without opening bottles.

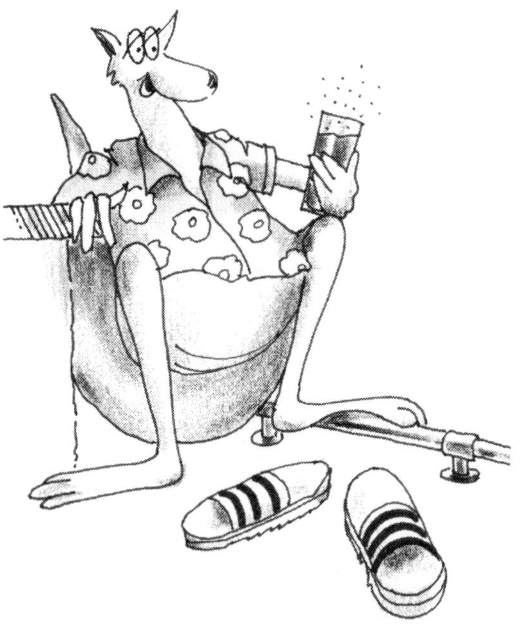

Winning Aussie Beer Recipes

These recipes are some of the best in Australia. Because they come from a variety of sources they do not follow our method to the letter. If in doubt follow our method – it will not harm the beer and occasionally may improve it.

We have converted every measure to work on a brew of 20 litres. Remember, the "so called" 5 gallon barrel is 22.270 litres – there is no exact equivalent and 20 litres is easy to divide and multiply into the quantity that suits you. All measures are metric with grammes translated into metric spoons for easy use.

We have also included low alcohol recipes for those who enjoy light beers.

McKENZIE LAGER

Medium strength with a nice crisp finish.

20 litres – Original Gravity 1.040

What you need –

lager malt extract	- 1.5 kg
crushed lager malt grain	- 200 g
pearl barley	- 100 g
white sugar	- 900 g
Pride of Ringwood	- 40 g (1⅓ cups)
Irish moss	- 5 g (1 tsp)
Epsom salts	- 2.5 g (½ tsp)
lager yeast	

What to do –

1. Heat water in pan to 60°C and stir in crushed malts and barley. Stir and raise mash temperature to 67°C. Switch off heat. Reheat and stir occasionally to maintain 67°C for 1½ hours.
2. Using hotter water, sparge by rinsing grains.
3. Boil this extract, with lager malt extract, Epsom salts, 20 g hops for 1 hour.
4. Add 10 g hops, continue to boil for 20 minutes.
5. Add 10 g hops and Irish moss, continue to boil for 10 minutes. Stop boil.
6. Dissolve sugar in hot water, add to main boil.
7. Strain wort into 20 ltr container. Wash hops with hot water, add to container. Top up with cold water.
8. Allow wort to reach room temperature, check O.G. and add yeast.
9. Allow to work for three days. Siphon into final fermenter, under airlock. Add finings and bottle when S.G. under 1.008.

SOUTHERN CROSS LAGER

A tangy darker lager with more body.

20 litres – O.G. 1.045

What you need –

crushed pale malt	- 1.25 kg
crushed lager malt	- 1 kg
glucose	- 225 g
Saaz hop pellets	- 30 g
Epsom salts	- 2.5 g (½ tsp)
lager yeast	
Irish moss	- 5 g (1 tsp)

What to do –

1. Heat water in pan to 60°C and stir in crushed malts. Stir and raise mash temperature to 67°C. Switch off heat. Reheat and stir occasionally to maintain 67°C for 1½ hours.
2. Using hotter water, sparge by rinsing grains.
3. Boil this extract with Epsom salts, glucose and 15 g hops for 1 hour.
4. Add 8 g hops, continue to boil for 20 minutes.
5. Add 7 g hops and Irish moss, continue to boil for 10 minutes. Stop boil.
6. Strain wort into 20 ltr container. Wash hops with hot water, add to container. Top up with cold water.
7. Allow wort to reach room temperature, check O.G. and add yeast.
8. Allow to work for three days. Siphon into final fermenter, under airlock. Add finings and bottle when S.G. under 1.008.

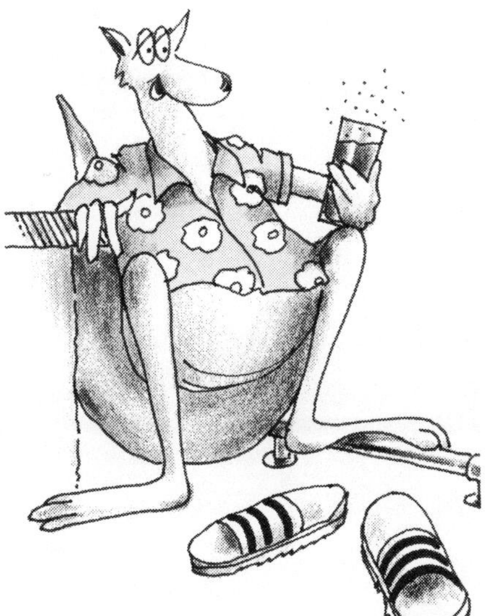

MUNICH LAGER

A simple light lager with good colour.
20 litres – Original Gravity 1.035

What you need –

pale malt extract	- 1.5 kg
Raw sugar	- 2 kg
Saaz hop pellets	- 20 g
Irish moss	- 5 g (1 tsp)
Epsom salts	- 2.5 g (½ tsp)
lager yeast	

What to do –

1. Boil malt extract, Epsom salts, 10 g hops for 1 hour.
2. Add 5 g hops, continue to boil for 20 minutes.
3. Add 5 g hops and Irish moss, continue to boil for 10 minutes. Stop boil.
4. Dissolve sugar in hot water and add to main boil.
5. Strain wort into 20 litre container. Wash hops with hot water, add to container. Top up with cold water.
6. Allow wort to work for three days. Siphon into final fermenter, under airlock. Add finings and bottle when S.G. under 1.008.

PREMIUM LAGER

Lightly flavoured with a refreshing bite.

20 litres – Original Gravity 1.040

What you need –

crushed lager malt grain	- 1.8 kg
White sugar	- 800 g
Hallertau hop pellets	- 40g
Irish moss	- 5 mls (1 tsp)
lager yeast	

What to do –

1. Heat water in pan to 60 °C and stir in crushed malts. Stir and raise mash temperature to 67 °C. Switch off heat. Reheat and stir occasionally to maintain 67 °C for 1-1½ hours.
2. Using hotter water, sparge by rinsing grains.
3. Boil this extract with 20 g of hops for 1 hour.
4. Add 10 g hops, continue to boil for 20 minutes.
5. Add 10 g hops and Irish moss, continue to boil for 10 minutes. Stop boil.
6. Dissolve sugar in hot water and add to main boil.
7. Strain wort into 20 litre container. Wash hops with hot water, add to container. Top up with cold water.
8. Allow wort to reach room temperature, check O.G. and add yeast.
9. Allow to work for three days. Siphon into final fermenter under airlock. Add finings and bottle when S.G. under 1.008. Prime with brown sugar.

PILSENER LAGER

A smooth refreshing lager with a nice head.

20 litres – Original Gravity 1.035

What you need –

crushed lager malt grain	- 2.3 kg
Flaked barley	- 400 g
Hallertau hop pellets	- 30 g
Irish moss	- 5 mls (1 tsp)
brewers caramel	- 2 mls
lager yeast	

What to do -

1. Heat water in pan to 60°C and stir in crushed malt, Brewers caramel and flaked Barley. Stir and raise mash temperature to 67°C. Switch off heat. Reheat and stir occasionally to maintain 6°C for 1-1½ hours.
2. Using hotter water, sparge by rinsing grains.
3. Boil this extract with 15 g of hops for 1 hour.
4. Add 7 g hops, continue to boil for 20 minutes.
5. Add 8 g hops and Irish moss, continue to boil for 10 minutes. Stop boil.
6. Strain wort into 20 litre container. Wash hops with hot water, add to container. Top up with cold water.
7. Allow wort to reach room temperature, check O.G. and add yeast.
8. Allow to work for three days. Siphon into final fermenter under airlock. Add finings and bottle when S.G. under 1.008.

SCHOONER DRAUGHT

Lightly flavoured Australian style draught

20 litres – Original Gravity 1.040

What you need –

amber malt extract	- 1.5 kg
glucose	- 600 g
Saaz hop pellets	- 20 g
Epsom salts	- 2 g (½ tsp)

Irish moss	- 5 g (1 tsp)
lager yeast	

What to do –

1. Boil malt extract, glucose, 10 g hops, Epsom salts for 1 hour.
2. Add 5 g hops, continue to boil for 20 minutes.
3. Add 5 g hops and Irish moss and continue to boil for 10 minutes. Stop boil.
4. Strain wort into 20 litre container. Wash hops with hot water and add to container. Top up with cold water.
5. Allow wort to reach room temperature, check O.G. and add yeast.
6. Allow to work for three days. Siphon into final fermenter, under airlock. Add finings and bottle when S.G. under 1.008.

X'S SPECIAL LIGHT ALE

A lighter refreshingly bitter ale.

20 litres – O.G. 1.035

What you need –

lager malt extract	- 1.5 kg
Dextrose Monohydrate	- 1 kg
Fuggles hop pellets	- 25 g
crushed crystal malt	- 250 g
Irish moss	- 2.5 g
brewers yeast	

What to do –

1. Boil the malt extract, malt grain and hops in water for 45 minutes. Carefully strain off the wort from hops and grain into container.
2. Using hotter water, sparge by rinsing grains.
3. Dissolve the Dextrose Monohydrate in hot water and add to boil. Top up with cold water.
4. Allow wort to reach room temperature. Check O.G. and add yeast.
5. Allow to work for three days. Siphon into final fermenter under airlock. Add finings and bottle when S.G. under 1.008.

INDIA PALE ALE

This delightful beer is somewhere between a lager and a light ale, with the best qualities of both.

20 litres – O.G. 1.040

What you need –

crushed pale malt grain	- 2.5 kg
brown sugar	- 450 g
Irish moss	- 5 mls (1 tsp)
brewers caramel	- 2.5 mls (½ tsp)
Goldings hop pellets	- 25 g
lager yeast	

What you do –

1. Heat water in pan to 60°C and stir in crushed malt and brewers caramel. Stir and raise mash temperature to 67°C. Switch off heat. Reheat and stir occasionally to maintain 67°C for 1½ hours.
2. Using hotter water, sparge by rinsing grains.
3. Boil this extract with 15 g of hops for 1 hour.
4. Add 5 g hops, continue to boil for 20 minutes.
5. Add 5 g hops and Irish moss, continue to boil for 10 minutes. Stop boil.
6. Dissolve sugar in hot water, add to main boil.
7. Strain wort into 20 litre container. Wash hops with hot water, add to container. Top up with cold water.
8. Allow wort to reach room temperature. Check O.G. and add yeast.
9. Allow to work for three days. Siphon into final fermenter, under airlock. Add finings and bottle when S.G. under 1.008.

COLONIAL LIGHT BITTER

A lightly coloured, lightly flavoured draught. Also known as the Woolshed Welcome.

20 litres – Original Gravity 1.037

What you need –

crushed pale malt grains	- 2 kg
crushed crystal malt	- 75 g
white sugar	- 450 g
Golding hop pellets	- 35 g

Irish moss	- 5 g (1 tsp)
brewers yeast	

What you do –

1. Heat water in pan to 60°C and stir in crushed malt. Stir and raise mash temperature to 67°C. Switch off heat. Reheat and stir occasionally to maintain 67°C for total of 1½ hours.
2. Using hotter water, sparge by rinsing grains.
3. Boil this extract with 15 g hops for 1 hour.
4. Add 10 g hops, continue to boil for 20 minutes.
5. Add 10 g hops and Irish moss, continue to boil for 10 minutes. Stop boil.
6. Dissolve sugar in hot water, add to main boil.
7. Strain wort into 20 litre container. Top with cold water.
8. Allow wort to reach room temperature, check O.G. and add yeast.
9. Allow to work for three days. Siphon into final fermenter under airlock. Add finings and bottle when S.G. below 1.008.

TASMAN BITTER

A medium draught beer with great colour and aroma.

20 litres – Original Gravity 1.040

What you need –

amber malt extract	- 1.5 kg
crushed porter malt grain	- 100 g
crushed crystal malt grain	- 50 g
brown sugar	- 700 g
lactose	- 200 g
Hallertau hop pellets	- 20 g
Irish moss	- 5 g (1 tsp)
brewers yeast	

What to do –

1. Heat water in pan to 60°C and stir in crushed malt grains. Stir and raise mash temperature to 67°C. Switch off heat. Reheat and stir occasionally to maintain temperature for 1½ hours.
2. Using hotter water, sparge by rinsing grains.
3. Boil this extract with 20 g of hops for 1 hour.
4. Add 10 g hops, continue to boil for 20 minutes.
5. Add 10 g hops and Irish moss, continue to boil for 10 minutes. Stop boil.

6. Dissolve sugar and lactose in hot water and add to main boil.
7. Strain wort into 20 litre container. Wash hops with hot water, add to container. Top up with cold water.
8. Allow wort to reach room temperature, check O.G. and add yeast.
9. Allow to work for three days. Siphon into final fermenter under airlock. Fine, then bottle when S.G. under 1.008.

WESTERN BROWN ALE

An Australian hoppy beer that's lighter and more refreshing than its name would lead you to imagine.

20 litres – Original Gravity 1.044

What you need –

crushed pale malt	- 2.3 kg
flaked barley	- 300 g
Dextrose Monohydrate	- 500 g
Irish moss	- 5 g (1 tsp)
Hallertau hop pellets	- 35 g
lager yeast	

What to do –

1. Heat water in pan to 60°C and stir in malt and barley. Stir and raise mash temperature to 67°C. Switch off heat. Reheat and stir occasionally to maintain temperature at 67°C for 1½ hours.
2. Using hotter water, sparge by rinsing grains.
3. Boil this extract with 20 g of hops for 1 hour.
4. Add 7 g hops, continue to boil for 20 minutes.
5. Add 8 g hops and Irish moss, continue to boil for 10 minutes. Stop boil.
6. Dissolve Dextrose in hot water and add to main boil.
7. Strain wort into 20 litre container. Wash hops with hot water, add to container. Top up with cold water.
8. Allow wort to reach room temperature. Check O.G. and add yeast.
9. Allow to work for three days. Siphon into final fermenter under airlock. Add finings and bottle when S.G. under 1.008.

ANZAC BITTER

Enjoyable hoppy draught with extra flavour from roasted malts.

20 litres – Original Gravity 1.033

What you need –

crushed pale malt	- 2.0 kg
flaked barley	- 150 g
crushed black malt	- 100 g
Dextrose Monohydrate	- 400 g
caramel	- 5 mls (1 teaspoon)
Irish moss	- 5 g (1 teapsoon)
Fuggles hop pellets	- 35 g
Brewers yeast	

What to do –

1. Heat water in pan to 60°C and stir in crushed pale malt barley and black malt grains. Stir and raise mash temperature to 67°C. Switch off heat. Reheat and stir occasionally to maintain temperature at 67°C for 1½ hours.
2. Using hotter water, sparge by rinsing grains.
3. Boil total extract with 20 g hops for 1 hour.
4. Add 7 g hops, continue to boil for 20 minutes.
5. Add 8 g hops and Irish moss, continue to boil for 10 minutes.
6. Dissolve Dextrose in hot water and add to main boil.
7. Strain wort into 20 litre container. Top up with cold water.
8. Allow wort to reach room temperature, check O.G. and add yeast.
9. Allow to work for three days. Siphon into final fermenter under airlock, add finings and bottle when S.G. under 1.008. Prime with brown sugar.

OLD BREWERY BEST BITTER

A traditional English beer. Full bodied and malty. Try it really cold.

20 litres – O.G. 1.045

What you need –

crushed pale malt	- 2.25 kg
glucose	- 450 g
crushed crystal malt	- 125 g
flaked rice	- 100 g
Golding hop pellets	- 35 g
demerara sugar	- 75 g
Irish moss	- 5 g (1 tsp)
brewers yeast (top fermenting)	

What to do –

1. Heat water in pan to 60°C and stir in malt and rice. Stir and raise mash temperature to 67°C. Switch off heat. Reheat and stir occasionally to maintain temperature at 67°C for 1½ hours.
2. Using hotter water, sparge by rinsing grains.
3. Boil total extract with 20 g of hops for 1 hour.
4. Add 8 g of hops and continue to boil for 20 minutes.
5. Add 7 g of hops and Irish moss and continue to boil for 10 minutes. Stop boil.
6. Dissolve demerara sugar in hot water - add to main boil.
7. Strain wort into 20 litre container. Wash hops with hot water, add to container. Top up with cold water.
8. Allow wort to reach room temperature. Check O.G. and add yeast.
9. Allow to work for three days. Siphon into final fermenter under airlock. Add finings and bottle when S.G. under 1.008. Prime with brown sugar.

IRON MAN ALE

An elephant-sized alcohol-by-volume beer. About as strong as an ale can be. Enjoyable, but treat with caution!

20 litres – O.G. 1.060

What you need –

amber malt extract	- 1.5 kg
crystal malt grains	- 750 g
Hallertau hop pellets	- 45 g
brown sugar	- 1.5 kg
white sugar	- 2.0 kg
Irish moss	- 5 g
beer yeast – top fermenter	

What to do –

1. Heat water in pan to 60°C and stir in crushed crystal malt grains. Stir and raise mash temperature to 67°C. Switch off heat. Reheat and stir occasionally to maintain temperature at 67°C for 1½ hours.
2. Using hotter water, sparge by rinsing grains.
3. Boil this extract with 20 g of hops for 1 hour.
4. Add 15 g hops, continue to boil for 20 minutes.
5. Add 10 g hops and Irish moss, continue to boil for 10 minutes. Stop boil.
6. Dissolve sugar in hot water and add to main boil.
7. Strain wort into 20 litre container. Wash hops with hot water, add to container. Top up with cold water.
8. Allow wort to reach room temperature, check O.G. and add yeast.
9. Allow to work for three days. Siphon into final fermenter under airlock. Add finings and bottle when S.G. under 1.008. Prime with brown sugar.

TOBY JUG STOUT

A traditional full-flavoured full-bodied English Stout.

20 litres – O.G. 1.045

What you need –

crushed pale malt	- 2.5 kg
crushed roasted barley	- 225 g
crushed black malt	- 100 g
golden syrup	- 4 dessertspoonsful
Pride of Ringwood hops	- 40 g
lactose	- 250 g
brewers yeast	

What to do –

1. Heat water in pan to 60°C and stir in crushed malt and barley. Stir and raise mash temperature to 67°C. Switch off heat. Reheat and stir occasionally to maintain temperature at 67°C for 2½ hours.
2. Using hotter water, sparge by rinsing grains.
3. Boil total extract with 20 g of hops for 1 hour.
4. Add 10 g hops, continue to boil for 20 minutes.
5. Add 10 g hops and Irish moss, continue to boil for 10 minutes. Stop boil.
6. Dissolve lactose and golden syrup in hot water and add to main boil.
7. Strain wort into 20 litre container. Wash hops with hot water, add to container. Top up with cold water.
8. Allow wort to reach room temperature, check O.G. and add yeast.
9. Allow to work for three days. Siphon into final fermenter under airlock. Add finings and bottle when S.G. under 1.008. Prime with brown sugar.

COUNTRY BARREL STOUT

A simple, lighter stout that's as easy to make as it is to drink.

20 litres – Original Gravity 1.045

What you need –

stout malt extract	- 2 kg
Irish moss	- 5 g (1 tsp)
soft brown sugar	- 2 kg
Fuggels hop pellets	- 20 g
lactose	- 100 g
brewers yeast	

What to do –

1. Boil Malt extract in water for 1 hour with 15 g of hops.
2. After 20 minutes, add Irish moss and 5 g of hops.
3. Add soft brown sugar dissolved in hot water.
4. Strain wort into 20 litre container, wash hops with hot water and add to container. Top up with cold water.
5. Allow wort to reach room temperature, check O.G. and add yeast.

6. Allow to work for three days. Siphon into final fermenter, under airlock. Add finings and bottle when S.G. under 1.008. Prime with brown sugar.

POWERHOUSE BARLEY STOUT

Possibly the strongest beer brewed in the world. Also called a "meal in a glass" but better known as Black Doom. A smooth, smooth wine strength stout.

20 litres – Original Gravity 1.103

What you need –

crushed pale malt	- 6 kg
crushed crystal malt	- 500 g
flaked barley	- 250 g
crushed black malt grain	- 250 g
brown sugar	- 1 kg
Pride of Ringwood hops	- 200 g
Irish moss	- 5 g (1 tsp)
all purpose wine yeast	

What to do –

1. Heat water in pan to 60°C and stir in crushed malt grains and barley. Stir and raise mash temperature to 67°C. Switch off heat. Reheat and stir occasionally to maintain temperature at 67°C for 1½ hours.
2. Using hotter water, sparge by rinsing grains.
3. Boil total extract with 100 g of hops for 1 hour.
4. Add 50 g hops, continue to boil for 20 minutes.
5. Add 50 g hops and Irish moss, continue to boil for 10 minutes. Stop boil.
6. Dissolve brown sugar in hot water and add to main boil.
7. Strain wort into 20 litre container. Wash hops with hot water, add to container. Top up with cold water.
8. Allow wort to reach room temperature, check O.G. and add wine yeast.
9. Allow to work for three days. Siphon into final fermenter under airlock. Depending on the temperature, 16°C - 18°C is ideal, this beer will take months to be ready for bottling. Do not fine, a little sediment will assist the brown priming sugar in each bottle. Wait six months before drinking. Worth the wait.

LOW ALCOHOL BEERS

The low alcohol beers you see in bottle shops have been made by a very complex brewing process that begins with a full beer and reduces the alcohol to retain as much of the beer taste as possible. It is a process you cannot hope to duplicate at home. However, there are ways to control the Original Gravity to determine the final percentage of alcohol to volume in the finished beer.

Our calculations in this book include the priming sugar. It is most unlikely the beer will ferment out totally, so practically speaking you will most likely create a beer below the alcohol-by-volume potentially possible. About the best compromise we could develop, between low alcohol and beer taste, is in the region of a potential 1.7% alcohol by volume. This compares very favourably with the normal commercial beer of 4% upward, and stronger home brews. Remember, you are unlikely to reach even this 1.7%.

LOW-ALCOHOL LAGER, BITTER & STOUT

These recipes may seem a little light on the number of ingredients. This is simply because most brewing ingredients contribute towards the alcohol content of the beer. We have attempted to keep to the spirit of home brewing (the beer will be better than our bad jokes) and give you all the beer taste, tang and refreshing qualities you want to enjoy. Low-alcohol brewing is no headache if you use your hydrometer carefully.

LOW-ALCOHOL LAGER

RECIPE 1 – 20 litres – O.G. 1.010

lager malt extract	- 500 g
Saaz hop pellets	- 30 g
Irish moss	- 5 g
lager yeast	

Prime with brown sugar. Use Malt Extract method described on Page 36.

LOW ALCOHOL BITTER

RECIPE 1 – 20 litres – O.G. 1.010

amber malt extract	- 600 g
Hallertau hop pellets	- 20 g
Irish moss	- 5 g
brewers yeast	

Brown sugar to bring Original Gravity to 1.010. Prime with brown sugar. Use Malt Extract method described on Page 36.

RECIPE 2 – 20 litres – O.G. 1.010

crushed pale malt	- 900 g
crushed black malt	- 50 g
Hallertau hop pellets	- 20 g
Irish moss	- 5 g
brewers yeast	

Brown sugar to bring Original Gravity to 1.010. Prime with brown sugar. Use Malted Grain method described on Page 37.

LOW ALCOHOL STOUT

RECIPE 1 – 20 litres – O.G. 1.010

stout malt extract	- 600 g
Pride of Ringwood hops	- 40 g
lactose	- 100 g
licorice	- 30 g
Irish moss	- 5 g
brewers yeast	

Brown sugar to bring Original Gravity to 1.010. Add licorice at beginning of main boil. Use Malt Extract method as described on Page 36. Prime with brown sugar.

RECIPE 2 – 20 litres – O.G. 1.010

crushed pale malt	- 800 g
crushed black malt	- 200 g
lactose	- 100 g
licorice	- 30 g
Irish moss	- 5 g
Fuggles hop pellets	- 20 g
brewers yeast	

Brown sugar to bring Original Gravity to 1.010. Add licorice at beginning of main boil. Use Malted Grain method as described on Page 37. Prime with brown sugar.

HOW TO BREW FAMOUS BEERS FROM AROUND THE WORLD

As you would expect, the great brewers of the world guard their secrets. They have invested millions in equipment and have spent years perfecting the taste that has made them famous. We cannot exactly duplicate their beers at home, but we can get mighty close. The really dedicated brewer should buy the original, enjoy the contents and refill with his own version of the beer, then test the palate of friends.

You will notice that in many cases the brewing method is different from the system followed in the vast majority of recipes. These beers are generally lighter and more delicately flavoured and require special treatment.

IMITATION "BUDWEISER" – U.S.A.

The largest selling beer in the world. This recipe will show you why.

2 litres – O.G. 1.046

You will need –

crushed lager malt	- 2.8 kg
Flaked rice	- 650 g
Irish moss	- 5 g
Hallertau hop pellets	- 25 g
lager yeast	

What to do –

1. Heat water in pan and stir in crushed malt and rice. Then raise temperature to 67 °C. Switch off heat. Reheat and stir occasionally to main temperature at 67 °C for 2 hours.
2. Using hotter water, sparge by rinsing grains.
3. Boil total extract with 15 g hops for 1 hour.
4. Add 5 g hops, continue to boil for 20 minutes.
5. Add 5 g hops and Irish moss, continue to boil for 10 minutes.

6. Strain wort into 20 litre container. Wash hops with hot water, add to fermenter. Top up with cold water.
7. Allow wort to reach room temperature, check O.G. and add yeast. Add finings and bottle when S.G. under 1.008. Prime with white sugar.

IMITATION "LOWENBRAU"

According to law only barley, hops and water can be used to brew beer in Germany. It is pure beer and a pure pleasure to drink.

20 litres – O.G. 1.060

You will need –

crushed lager malt	- 5 kg
crushed crystal malt	- 80 g
Irish moss	- 5 g
Hallertau hop pellets	- 15 g
Saaz hop pellets	- 30 g
lager yeast	

What to do –

1. Heat water in pan to 40°C and stir in crushed malt. Stir and raise mash temperature to 50°C. Let it stand for ½ hour. Raise temperature to 67°C. Switch off heat. Reheat and stir occasionally to maintain temperature at 67°C for 1½ hours.
2. Using hotter water, sparge by rinsing grains.
3. Boil with all Hallertau hops and all Saaz hops for 1½ hours. Switch off heat, add Irish moss.
4. Strain into 20 litre container. Wash hops in hot water and add to fermenter. Top up with cold water.
5. Allow wort to reach room temperature, check O.G. and add yeast. Add finings and bottle when S.G. under 1.008. Prime with white sugar.

IMITATION "HEINEKEN" – HOLLAND

A beautiful lager with a great hop bite now brewed and enjoyed all over the world.

20 litres – O.G. 1.064

You will need –

crushed lager malt	- 1.5 kg
flaked rice	- 350 g
crushed crystal malt	- 80 g
Irish moss	- 5 g
Hallertau hop pellets	- 30 g
lager yeast	

What to do –

1. Heat water in pan and stir in flaked rice and crushed malts. Stir and raise mash temperature to 67 °C. Switch off heat. Reheat and stir occasionally to maintain temperature at 67 °C for 1½ hours.
2. Using hotter water, sparge by rinsing grains.
3. Boil total extract with 15 g of hops for 1 hour.
4. Add 8 g hops, continue to boil for 20 minutes.
5. Add 7 g hops and Irish moss, continue to boil for 10 minutes.
6. Strain wort into 20 litre container, wash hops with hot water and add to container. Top up with cold water.
7. Allow wort to reach room temperature, check O.G. and add yeast. Add finings and bottle when S.G. under 1.008. Prime with white sugar.

IMITATION "SAN MIGUEL" – SPAIN

Wherever in the world they speak Spanish you will find San Miguel. Pronounced San Mig-el when sober.

20 litres – O.G. 1.045

You will need –

lager brew can	- 1.8 kg
golden syrup	- 1 kg
Hallertau hop pellets	- 7 g
lager yeast	

What to do –

1. Simmer hops in pot for 15 minutes and pour liquid into final fermenter.
2. Add lager brew can and golden syrup.

3. Pour over 3 litres of hot water and stir to dissolve.
4. Top up with cold water. Add yeast.
5. Bottle when S.G. under 1.008. Prime with white sugar.

Weights & Measures

TO CONVERT	INTO	MULTIPLY BY
Pounds	Kilogrammes	.45359
Ounces	Grammes	28.3496
Grains	Grammes	.0648
Gallons	Litres	4.54596
Pints	Litres	.5683
Pints	Millilitres or Cubic centimetres	568.26
Fluid ounces	Millilitres or Cubic centimetres	28.413
Kilogrammes	Pounds	2.2046
Grammes	Ounces	.035274
Grammes	Grains	15.432
Litres	Gallons	.22
Litres	Pints	1.7598
Cubic Centrimetres or millilitres	Fluid ounces	.036
Fahrenheit	Centigrade	Subtract 32, multiply by 5, divide by 9.
Centigrade	Fahrenheit	Multiply by 9, divide by 5, and add 32.

WEIGHT CONVERSIONS

British to Metric

5 lb = 2.267 kilogrammes
4 lb = 1.814 kilos
3 lb = 1.360 kilos
2 lb = 907 grammes
1 lb = 453 g
½ lb = 226 g
¼ lb = 113 g
1 oz = 30 g (approx.)
½ oz = 15 g (approx.) Tablespoon
¼ oz = 8 g (approx.) Dessertspoon
⅛ oz = 4 g (approx.) Teaspoon

Metric to British

5 kilogrammes	=	11 lb
4 kilos	=	8 lb 12 oz
3 kilos	=	6 lb 9 oz
2 kilos	=	4 lb 6 oz
1 kilo	=	2 lb 3 oz
500 grammes	=	1 lb 1½ oz
250 g	=	8¾ oz
125 g	=	4½ oz
100 g	=	3½ oz
50 g	=	1¾ oz

CAPACITY CONVERSIONS

British to Metric

1 gallon	=	4.546 litres
	=	4546 millilitres (or c.c.s.)
1 pint	=	568 ml/cc
½ pint	=	284 ml/cc
1 fl oz	=	28 ml/cc
½ fl oz	=	15 ml/cc (Tablespoon)
¼ fl oz	=	10 ml/cc (Dessertspoon)
⅛ fl oz	=	5 ml/cc (Teaspoon)

Metric to British

5 litres	=	8 pints 14 oz
4½ litres	=	7 pints 18 oz
4 litres	=	7 pints
3 litres	=	5 pints 5 oz
2 litres	=	3 pints 10 oz
1 litre	=	1 pint 14 oz
500 millilitres	=	17 oz
250 ml/cc	=	8½ oz
125 ml/cc	=	4¼ oz
100 ml/cc	=	3½ oz
50 ml/cc	=	1¾ oz

Brew Talk

ALCOHOL

A complex substance that makes life worth living.

AEROBIC FERMENTATION

The initial stages of fermentation, when the beer uses free oxygen in the top of the fermenter and in the water.

ANAEROBIC FERMENTATION

The continuation of the fermentation process under an airlock, when the yeast is forced to degrade the sugars in the wort to obtain its oxygen.

CARBON DIOXIDE

The by-product of fermentation. It creates a protective blanket over the fermenting beer and is forced by its own pressure through the airlock.

FINING

Removing suspended solids that cause haze in new beer.

GRIST

All other grains except barley, used in brewing.

LEES

The dead yeast cells and other debris that collect at the bottom of the fermenter during fermentation.

HYDROMETER

Measures sugar content in unfermented beer, and the residual sugar in a finished beer.

PRIMING

Adding sugar to give the beer a head and sparkle in the bottle or keg.

RACK

Siphoning the beer from the lees.

SPARGING

Washing the sugar out of the grains.

SULPHITE

Using Metabisulphite to clean and sterilize.

WORT

The sweet mixture ready for fermentation.

YEAST

The brewer's friend, Saccharomycus cerevisiae.

XTREMELY ANGRY

The home brewer's partner if the kitchen is not properly cleaned after a combined brewing and quality control session.